SAN ANTONIO
I M P R E S S I O N S

PHOTOGRAPHY BY LAURENCE PARENT

FARCOUNTRY
PRESS

Right: La Villita is a vibrant arts community housed in buildings listed on the National Register of Historic Places. Begun as a cluster of adobe huts for Mexican soldiers of the Alamo, the village evolved into an upscale neighborhood in the Victorian era, declined in the early twentieth century, and was restored in the 1940s.

Title page: Since 1980, the San Antonio Botanical Garden has delighted visitors with its thirty-three acres of seasonal displays, including this rose garden.

Front cover: San Antonio's famed River Walk is the site of numerous annual events and is a beloved gathering place for locals and visitors alike.

Back cover: This fresco painted on the ceiling of Mission Concepción in San Antonio Missions National Historical Park is believed to depict God as a *mestizo*, or person of mixed Spanish and American Indian blood. Frescos once covered the interior and exterior of the church. Today, however, only three of the mission's rooms feature remnants of these works of art from the mid-eighteenth century.

ISBN 10: 1-56037-450-0
ISBN 13: 978-1-56037-450-3

© 2007 by Farcountry Press
Photography © 2007 by Laurence Parent

For more information about our books, write Farcountry Press, P.O. Box 5630, Helena, MT 59604; call (800) 821-3874; or visit www.farcountrypress.com.

Created, produced, and designed in the United States.
Printed in China.

12   11   10   09   08   07   1   2   3   4   5   6

Left: San Antonio Missions National Historical Park protects four missions dating from the early 1700s—all with active parishes. Here, against the backdrop of an impending storm, stands Mission San José y San Miguel de Aguayo, called "Queen of the Missions."

Below: At Mission San Francisco de la Espada in San Antonio Missions National Historical Park, this dam diverts water for the *acequia* (irrigation ditch) that once irrigated the fields. The aqueduct system continues to supply water to the mission and its former farmlands.

Right: Texas' war for independence from Mexico started after Antonio López de Santa Anna declared himself dictator in 1835. Texians, as they were then called, captured this fort, the Alamo, in December 1835 and held it—even through a siege by Santa Anna and 5,000 of his men from February 23 to March 6, 1836. While these Texians awaited relief, rebels with Sam Houston on the Brazos River declared Texas independent on March 2. In the early hours of March 6, Santa Anna's forces overran the Alamo, killing all but about fifteen slaves, women, and children.

Below: This cenotaph honors the approximately 190 people killed defending the Alamo in 1835. No one knows the exact number killed because Santa Anna had their bodies burned. Texas' war for independence ended on April 21, 1836, with Sam Houston's victory over Santa Anna, where he used the battle cry "Remember the Alamo!"

Above: The Alamodome offers space for football games, conventions, and events ranging from revivals to dog shows.

Left: The San Antonio Spurs' Tony Parker lays up a shot against Erick Dampier of the Dallas Mavericks at the AT&T Center. The WNBA San Antonio Silver Stars also call this arena home.
PHOTO BY BILL BAPTIST/NBAE/GETTY IMAGES

Above: At 404 feet in height, the Tower Life Building downtown was San Antonio's tallest office building for sixty years after its completion in 1929.

Right: Rare winter snow blankets Mission Espíritu Santo in Goliad State Park. The mission was once the largest cattle ranch in Texas, supplying Spanish colonial settlements as far away as Louisiana.

Left: American and European art of the nineteenth and twentieth centuries has been on exhibit at the McNay Art Museum for half a century.

Below: The McNay's grounds are open to the public for twelve hours a day, offering tranquil spots such as this pond.

Right: The San Antonio River Walk is a two-and-a-half-mile walkway along the San Antonio River between the Municipal Auditorium and the King William Historic District.

Below: Cruise boats carry visitors past the sidewalk cafes, specialty shops, nightclubs, and hotels along the River Walk.

Above: The Basilica of the National Shrine of the Little Flower was completed by the Discalced Carmelite Friars in 1931, six years after the canonization of Saint Therese de Lisieux (1873–1897), the "Little Flower of Jesus."

Left: San Antonio Missions National Historical Park encompasses the Spanish missions of San José, Concepción, San Juan, and Espada, built in the early 1700s in part to discourage France's expansion westward from Louisiana. Pictured is Mission Concepción.

Right: The clock tower stands tall at Fort Sam Houston's Quadrangle. The fort, built in the late 1870s and holding more than 900 structures, is one of the nation's oldest army installations. Today its modern facilities are home to an Army medical training site.

Far right: This building at Fort Sam Houston, or "Fort Sam" as it is known locally, was the Commanding General's Quarters. Today it is called the Pershing House, named for General John J. Pershing, who lived here in 1917 before leading American troops in France during World War I.

Left: San Antonio Municipal Auditorium and Conference Center opened in 1926, memorializing World War I veterans. Fifty-three years later, the interior was gutted by fire. Featuring a renovated and modernized interior, and still housed in the elegant, historic structure, the auditorium reopened in 1985.

Below: Dedicated in 1968 by General William Westmoreland, the Vietnam Veterans Memorial outside the Municipal Auditorium portrays a radio operator comforting a fallen comrade while scanning the sky for the medevac helicopter he has summoned.

Above: Enchanted Springs Ranch near San Antonio is a town straight out of the Old West, with thirty buildings created for use as a movie and television set. Visitors also can watch exotic animals being trained for film and performance work.

Right: Less than an hour's drive from the city, Hill Country State Natural Area features forty miles of multi-use trails among live oaks, Ashe junipers, sotol plants, and many other plant species.

Left: In HemisFair Park, site of the 1968 World's Fair, Tower of the Americas includes a four-dimensional theater experience of flying over Texas sites and on the space shuttle; an observation deck; banquet and meeting space; and a revolving restaurant. At 750 feet in height, the tower stands 145 feet taller than Seattle's Space Needle and 195 feet taller than the Washington Monument.

Below: Jim Cullum, at left on cornet, leads his band in traditional jazz of the 1890s and early 1900s six nights a week at Jim Cullum's Jazz Landing restaurant and club on the River Walk.

Right: The intricate stone carving around Mission San José's Rose Window is an example of the style of carving found on many buildings at San Antonio Missions National Historical Park.

Facing page: Now restored, the mill at Mission San José in San Antonio Missions National Historical Park was used for grinding wheat in the early days.

Above: Located in the Mercado, Mi Tierra Restaurant and Bakery has served Tex-Mex cuisine since 1941. Begun as a three-table café, the restaurant now seats more than 500 and is open twenty-four hours a day.

Diners along the River Walk enjoy outdoor café seating along the San Antonio River.

Above: Choke Canyon Lake, in Choke Canyon State Park, is a water reservoir for Corpus Christi, but also features guided birdwatching walks, picnic sites, camping, softball and volleyball courts, horse trails, fishing, and boating.

Right: Sunset casts a warm glow on the Tower Life Building and other structures along the San Antonio River.

Above: Lucile Halsell Conservatory at San Antonio Botanical Garden displays a variety of plant life, from Hill Country wildflowers to palms, such as these.

Left: Designed by Emilio Ambasz, the San Antonio Botanical Garden's Conservatory comprises individual glass buildings that house specialty collections ranging from alpine plants to equatorial tropicals.

Above: Just south of downtown, South Alamo Street is the site for the city's monthly art walk, known as "First Friday," when street vendors sell their wares to the strolling crowds.

Right: San Antonio Museum of Art, housed in the reconfigured 1884 Lone Star Brewery, opened in 1981 to exhibit western antiquities, Asian art, Latin American art, and contemporary American paintings, sculpture, and decorative arts.

Left and below: Fiesta San Antonio is a ten-day cultural celebration and city-wide party held annually in April. Events are held indoors and out, with several parades (including one on the river), dances, sporting events, special museum exhibits, and plenty of music and food.

PHOTO BY BOB DAEMMRICH PHOTOGRAPHY, INC. (LEFT)

PHOTOS COURTESY OF RANDY BEAR, FIESTA SAN ANTONIO COMMISSION (BELOW, TOP AND BOTTOM)

Above: Native to the Arabian Peninsula, this Arabian oryx at the San Antonio Zoo and Aquarium is one of about 600 in captivity around the world. San Antonio's zoo developed from a herd of exotic animals given to the city in 1914 and has pioneered natural-habitat facilities for a variety of wild creatures.

Right: A herd of rhinoceroses, like these at the zoo, is not surprisingly called a "crash." The giant herbivores can grow to weigh more than a ton, live for about fifty years, and are endangered in their native Africa and Southeast Asia.

Following pages: Across the street from the Alamo, a variety of attractions offer visitors some less serious fare.

Above: Park interpreters at Casa Navarro State Historic Site in downtown San Antonio describe the life and times of Tejano-patriot José Antonio Navarro (1795–1871), who lived here. A signer of the Texas Declaration of Independence in 1836, Navarro served in Texas legislatures under Mexico and both the Republic and the State of Texas, and was a prominent rancher and merchant.

Left: Opened near the Alamo in 1859, the Menger Hotel has undergone expansions and renovations to maintain its position as a first-class hotel of every era. Near its Victorian lobby stands the James N. Muir sculpture *Colonel Travis: The Line*, which portrays the moment when Colonel William Travis legendarily informed his 186 men at the Alamo that those who stayed were doomed. Some say that all but one stepped across the line Travis drew in the sand after he demanded, "Those prepared to give their lives in freedom's cause, come over to me."

Above: For many years after its 1929 opening, the ornate Majestic Theatre stood as the second-largest motion picture venue in the nation, with 2,311 seats. It closed at the end of 1974 but was restored to its original design and reopened as a City of San Antonio property in 1989. Besides serving as the San Antonio Symphony's home, it hosts musical plays, concerts of all types, and other live performances.

Facing page: Sunset Station in downtown San Antonio is the renovated 1902 Southern Pacific Railroad Depot. Today it houses restaurants and serves as a venue for concerts, meetings, and other events.

Left and facing page: Mission San José and its cloisters offer many peaceful spots for contemplation.

Right and far right: Blue Star Contemporary Art Center was established by artists and volunteers in 1985, in a 1920s riverside warehouse, to support and exhibit the work of contemporary artists. Today it is the centerpiece for the Blue Star Arts Complex of apartments, art studios, galleries, and performance spaces.

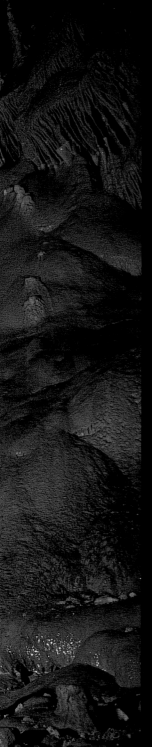

Above: Horse racing and pari-mutuel betting—including Kentucky Derby prelimi-
naries—have been available at Retama Park, in nearby Selma, since 1995.

PHOTO COURTESY OF COADY PHOTOGRAPHY

Left: North of San Antonio near New Braunfels is Natural Bridge Caverns, where
guides show off 10,000 underground formations. Pictured is the Cathedral Room
in South Cave.

Above and right: Shoppers find a variety of imported goods in the many shops of El Mercado at Market Square, the largest Mexican marketplace outside of Mexico.

Above: The congregation of San Fernando Cathedral in downtown San Antonio began with fifteen families who emigrated from the Canary Islands, invited by Spain's King Phillip V in 1731. The current building was completed in 1873, the year before Pope Pius IX named San Antonio a diocese.

Left: Inside and out, San Fernando is a fine example of French Gothic architecture as interpreted in the nineteenth century.

Right and facing page: The first mission in Texas, Mission Espada was founded in 1690 at today's town of Weches and was moved to the San Antonio River in 1731. The beautiful stone- and woodwork was completed twenty-five years later.

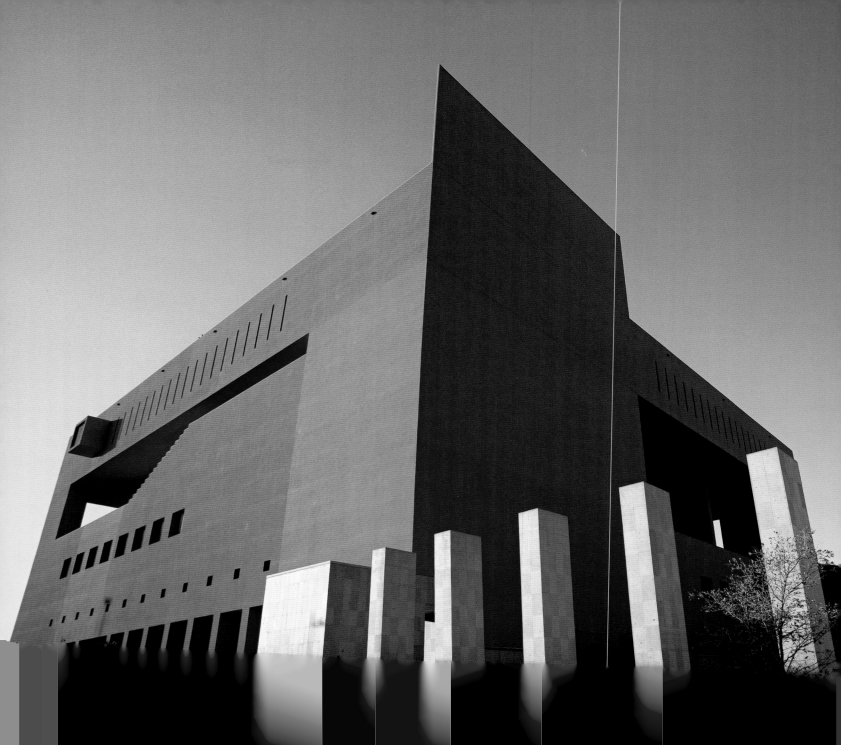

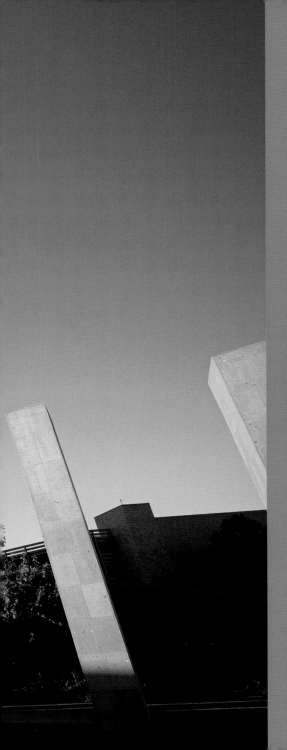

Above: Last light tints the tower of Bexar County Courthouse, which dates from 1929. With San Antonio as its seat, Bexar (pronounced "bear" in English) County took its name from the original presidio, or fort, that protected Mission San Antonio de Valero (later the Alamo) and was named for a son of the Spanish Duke of Béxar.

Left: In designing Central Library, a branch of the San Antonio Public Library system that opened in 1995, architect Ricardo Legorreta sought to create an inviting space where people gather and relax as well as read and research. "I wanted to break the concept that libraries are imposing," he has stated.

Above and right: Located along the River Walk, the Southwest School of Art and Craft occupies adjoining campuses, including the former Ursuline Academy and Convent founded in 1851 as a girls' academy. Seen here is the Ursuline chapel, a French Gothic structure begun in 1868.

Left: Framed by a mesquite tree is Mission Concepcíon, now part of San Antonio Missions National Historical Park. Dating from 1755, it is the oldest stone church in the United States that has never been restored.

Below: A quiet walkway in the Alamo recalls its founding in 1724 as Mission San Antonio de Valero, home for Spanish missionaries and their Indian converts. Spain secularized Texas missions in 1793, distributed their lands to the Indians, and began using this mission as the fort they called the Alamo, meaning "cottonwood tree."

Above: The Buckhorn Saloon, founded in 1881, now includes a museum annex featuring this collection of chairs made from the horns of Texas cattle.

Right: The Buckhorn still sports its hand-crafted bar of cherry wood and marble.

Above: The Spanish Governor's Palace, its construction begun in 1722, never served as the governor's residence but rather as a fort protecting Mission San Antonio de Valero (the Alamo). It later served as the seat of Spanish government for the Texas colony. Its ten rooms now hold period furnishings.

Left: The keystone above the Spanish Governor's Palace door shows the coat of arms of King Ferdinand VI, and the approaching conquistador was a gift from Spain.

Above: In the Alamo's plaza, a Christmas tree brightens the night.

Right: Traditional luminárias are part of Mission Espíritu Santo's Christmas decorations. Founded in 1722, the mission was moved to this site in 1749, destroyed by an 1886 hurricane, and reconstructed by the Civilian Conservation Corps in the 1930s.

Above: The Witte Museum's exhibits cover South Texas history, culture, and natural science, with changing art exhibits, prehistoric art, wildlife dioramas, and reconstructed historic homes on the grounds. This sculpture, *Mother and Child* by Charles Umlauf, was installed in 1960.

Left: The Witte's popular H-E-B Science Treehouse provides children and adults with interactive exhibits explaining scientific principles—and a great place to climb and explore.

Above, left: In late 1835, Benjamin Rush Milam joined a company of Texian soldiers fighting for independence and, when they planned to stop for winter rather than head for San Antonio, famously cried, "Who will go with Ben Milam into San Antonio?" Three hundred men did, and they wrested the town from Mexican control, although Milam was killed during the house-to-house fighting. This statue in Ben Milam Park was placed by the Daughters of the Republic of Texas.

Above, right: This nine-story-tall mural on the CHRISTUS Santa Rosa Children's Hospital portrays a guardian angel and her young charge. Seven colors on 2,000 tiles present *Spirit of Healing,* by Jesse Trevino (1946–), who lost his right hand in Vietnam and retrained himself to use his left in creating art with Latino themes.

Facing page: A trainer performs with SeaWorld San Antonio's local "Shamu," a killer whale that weighs about 400 pounds

Above: Louis Tussaud's Plaza Wax Museum is among the tourist attractions across from the Alamo.

Left: Offering a Mesoamerican fantasy, the Aztec Theater opened in 1926 with an orchestra, chorus girls, and a Wurlitzer organ to enhance its silent films. Today it has been restored architecturally and modernized technologically as Aztec On The River, each performance presenting a silent film and then a contemporary work on a giant screen. Free special-effects shows are offered in the lobby.

Above: In the King William District of historical homes—originally named for Kaiser Wilhelm by German immigrants who lived here—the Guenther House dates from 1860, when it was built for Carl Hilmar Guenther, founder of Pioneer Flour Mills. It now houses a restaurant and is open to the public for tours.

Facing page: The three-story limestone Edward Steves Homestead Museum, also in the King William District, was built in 1876 as the home of the Steves Lumber Company founder. Since 1954, the house and outbuildings have been a museum, with tours daily.

Edward Steves Homestead
Museum

San Antonio Conservation Society

Open Daily   10:00am - 4:15pm
Last Tour Begins at 3:30

Left: Mission San Juan Capistrano's church and other buildings were completed in 1756, but the congregation was founded in 1716 in eastern Texas. The mission and its self-sustaining farming and crafting community were abandoned because of declining population, epidemics, and attacks by local Indian tribes. It can be visited in San Antonio Missions National Historical Park.

Facing page: An agave stem is silhouetted against the Mission Espíritu Santo—originally Mission Nuestra Señora del Espíritu Santo de Zúñiga.

LAURENCE PARENT was born and raised in New Mexico. After receiving a petroleum engineering degree at the University of Texas at Austin in 1981, he practiced engineering for six years before becoming a full-time freelance photographer and writer specializing in landscape, travel, and nature subjects. His photos appear in numerous calendars. His many article and photo credits include *National Geographic Traveler*, *Outside*, *Backpacker*, *Newsweek*, and the *New York Times*. Laurence contributes regularly to regional publications such as *Texas Highways*, *Texas Monthly*, *New Mexico Magazine*, and *Texas Parks & Wildlife*. He has had more than thirty books published.

He makes his home in the Austin area with his wife Patricia and two children.

Right: Up close, bullet scars from 1836 can be seen on the Alamo's façade.